CREEP OUT

GHOST TOWNS

VALERIE BODDEN

CREATIVE C EDUCATION

Published by Creative Education
P.O. Box 227, Mankato, Minnesota 56002
Creative Education is an imprint of The Creative Company
www.thecreativecompany.us

Design and production by Chelsey Luther
Art direction by Rita Marshall
Printed in China

Photographs by Alamy (INTERFOTO, Joana Kruse), Dreams-
time (Andesign101, Chip Clark, Lvphotog1, Ingemar Magnusson,
Maryann Preisinger, Samystclair, Sergecrane, Upthebanner),
Getty Images (Carol Polich Photo Workshops, George Lepp,
Dominik Pabis, SERGEI SUPINSKY), National Geographic
Creative (DAVID HISER, PETE RYAN), Shutterstock (rui vale
sousa, Andreas Zerndl)

Library of Congress Cataloging-in-Publication Data
Names: Bodden, Valerie, author.
Title: Ghost towns / Valerie Bodden.
Series: Creep out.
Includes bibliographical references and index.
Summary: Feel goosebumps begin to form as this title explores
ghost towns around the world, surveying common ghost-town
features and creepy stories about these places.

Identifiers: LCCN 2016033588 / ISBN 978-1-60818-807-9
(hardcover) / ISBN 978-1-56660-855-8 (eBook)
Subjects: LCSH: 1. Ghost towns—Psychological aspects—Juvenile
literature. 2. Haunted places—Juvenile literature. 3. Parapsy-
chology—Juvenile literature.
Classification: LCC BF1461.B63 2017 / DDC 133.1/22—dc23

CCSS: RI.1.1, 2, 3, 4, 5, 6, 10; RI.2.1, 2, 3, 4, 5, 6, 7, 10; RI.3.1, 2, 3, 4, 5,
10; RF.1.1, 3, 4; RF.2.3, 4; RF.3.3, 4

First Edition HC 9 8 7 6 5 4 3 2 1

Table *of* Contents

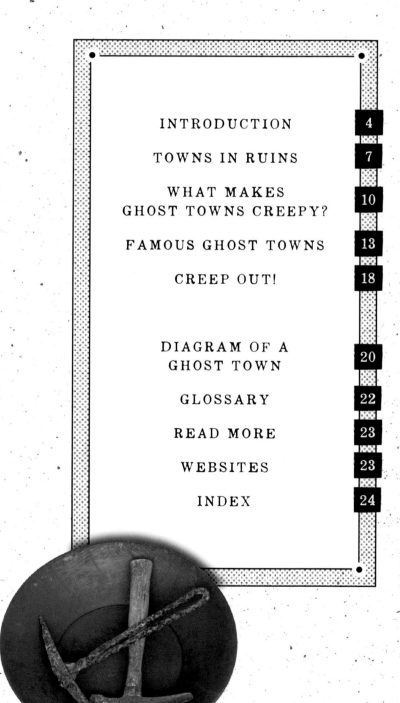

INTRODUCTION

EMPTY buildings surround you. Weeds grow in cracks. Wind moans through windows. You shiver, even though you are hot. This is a ghost town.

NO ONE HAS LIVED IN THIS GHOST TOWN IN MONTANA SINCE THE LATE 1930s.

TOWNS IN RUINS

A ghost town is deserted. The people who used to live there left. They might have left because of a disaster. Or maybe they needed to find new jobs.

DANGEROUS EXPLOSIONS AT POWER PLANTS CAN CAUSE PEOPLE TO LEAVE A TOWN.

PAGE
7

THE TOWN OF BANNACK IS KEPT
IN GOOD SHAPE BECAUSE IT IS
INSIDE A MONTANA STATE PARK.

Only a few ruins remain of some ghost towns. Others have many buildings. The buildings might look like they did when people lived there.

What Makes Ghost Towns Creepy?

GHOST towns creep some people out. Everything is empty and lonely. The only sounds are the wind and wild animals. Many ghost towns have old cemeteries. Some people think ghost towns are haunted.

AN EARTHQUAKE IN 1968 DROVE PEOPLE AWAY FROM THIS TOWN ON THE ISLAND OF SICILY.

Famous Ghost Towns

BODIE is a ghost town in California. More than 10,000 people once lived there. They came to mine gold. When the gold ran out, people left. Today, tourists visit the town. Some people think Bodie is cursed. People who take things from the town have bad luck.

BOTH BODIE (PICTURED) AND THE NEIGHBORING GHOST TOWN OF AURORA, NEVADA, CAN BE VISITED TODAY.

P OMPEII (*POM-pay*) was a city in Italy. In A.D. 79, a volcano erupted. It buried the city in ash. In the 1700s, people dug out part of the city. They found houses and buildings. Later, casts of the people who had died were made.

PLASTER WAS POURED OVER SKELETONS, LEFT TO HARDEN, AND THEN CHIPPED AWAY TO MAKE A CAST.

STRONG WINDS BLOW
THROUGH KOLMANSKOP,
PUSHING THE DESERT SAND
INTO OLD HOUSES.

KOLMANSKOP was a town in Namibia. It was built in 1908. People there mined for diamonds. After they dug up the diamonds, everyone left. Today, sand fills the buildings. Some say the town is haunted.

GHOST towns can be creepy day or night. You might feel all alone. But then you hear a strange sound. Will you get creeped out?

PLACES ALL AROUND THE WORLD HAVE BECOME GHOST TOWNS WHEN LOCAL MINES ARE CLOSED.

Diagram *of a* Ghost Town

STORES

Shelves are stocked and ready for people who never returned.

HITCHING POST

A good place to keep your horse while you explore.

HOMES

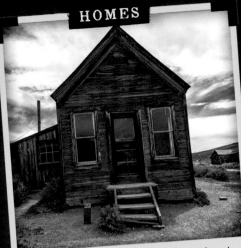

Sometimes the table is still set. Is someone coming back?

CEMETERY

A resting place for those who never left.

TUMBLEWEEDS

Wind pushes these balls of weeds down empty streets.

ROADS

Gunfights might have taken place here.

Glossary

CASTS—statues made by pouring cement or plaster into an opening and letting it harden into the shape of the opening

CURSED—something believed to have an evil spell on it

DESERTED—left empty and no longer used

DISASTER—something bad that happens suddenly and destroys many things, such as a flood or earthquake

TOURISTS—people who visit a place on a trip

Read More

Dicker, Katie. *Mysterious Places.* Mankato, Minn.: Smart Apple Media, 2015.

Michels, Troy. *The Lost City of Atlantis.* Minneapolis: Bellwether Media, 2011.

Websites

Bodie.com

http://www.bodie.com/
Check out pictures, videos, and facts about this famous ghost town.

Ghost Towns

http://www.ghosttowns.com/
Click on the map to see if there are any ghost towns near you.

⚠ Note: Every effort has been made to ensure that any websites listed above were active at the time of publication and suitable for children. However, because of the nature of the Internet, it is impossible to guarantee that these sites will remain active indefinitely or that their contents will not be altered.

Index